Barnesville Souvenir Coloring Book

by

Mike Duve

First Edition

This book celebrates the rich history of my hometown of Barnesville, Ohio. Inside, you will find 121 local street names, images of local landmarks, local festivals, local wildlife, and over 160 local businesses from Barnesville's past. Additionally, there are some totally abstract images, designed to challenge the devoted coloring book fan.

© 2017 All Rights Reserved

If you need copies of this book or if you would like a coloring book designed for YOUR business, please call or text the author at
740-213-3789

Make comments on our Facebook page.
Barnesville Ohio Coloring Book
www.facebook.com/barnesvillecoloringbook
fb.me/barnesvillecoloringbook
m.me/barnesvillecoloringbook

Individual pages available, if you want to have one colored and then framed, just contact me.

I am always looking for old photographs that can be turned into images for future editions of this coloring book.

Please let me know if you have something we can add in the future.

Show off your work!

When you color a page, take a picture with your phone and send it to my phone 740-213-3789 or post it on the facebook page "Barnesville Ohio Coloring Book"   or email it to me and I will post it. michealduve56@gmail.com

WELCOME TO THE BARNESVILLE SOUVENIR COLORING BOOK ENJOY

Barnesville is named after James Barnes, who was the first settler. Barnes was born in Montgomery County, Maryland and was married to Nancy Harrison.

In 1803, he moved to Ohio, settling first in

St. Clairsville, where he operated a tavern and general store.

In 1806 Barnes settled in Warren Township, Belmont County and cleared away the forest and built a house. He established a tannery and general store and planted orchards.

In November 1808, the town of Barnesville was laid out. Four years later, Mr. Barnes and his family became permanent residents of the new village.

Barnesville was described in 1833 as having six stores and a steam mill.

Barnesville was incorporated as a village in 1835.

A railroad was placed through the town in 1857, leading to what would be Barnesville's population boom.

The B&O Railroad built the town a much-needed depot in 1917. The railway brought with it industrialization and population growth. Watt Car and Wheel Company, the Eastern Ohio Glass Company, Hanlon Paper Company and the Barnesville Glass Company are some of the many manufacturing companies which moved into Barnesville during this time.

The Barnesville Baltimore & Ohio Depot is now 100 years old! Completed in 1917, this Spanish Mission-influenced brick building served as the "front door" for Barnesville, providing travel, shipment of produce, and delivery of goods. During the Civil War, this route was the main supply line for troops between the west and east theaters of war. In the fall of 1863, residents witnessed the first mass movement of troops by rail during wartime with over 20,000 men, mules, guns, and supplies being moved past this location. In fact, soldiers of western Belmont County left to serve from World War 1 to early in the Vietnam war from these doors.

The Depot building remains in excellent condition and is considered one of the few and finest examples left on the former B & O corridor. Its original clay tile roof is still in place, but is now in need of major repairs. The last winter was a tough one and the first rains of the season have brought serious leaking in several places. Without repair, major structural damage will occur to this magnificent building. In order to preserve the character of this historic treasure, the tiles will be numbered and removed one at a time, any necessary repairs made, replacement of the underlying weather protective layer, followed by reinstallation of the tiles to their original positions.
The bid for the project, including lumber for structural repairs, is in the ballpark of $150,000.

Your donation will help us replace this roof to secure the Barnesville B & O Depot, a piece of our history, for future generations.

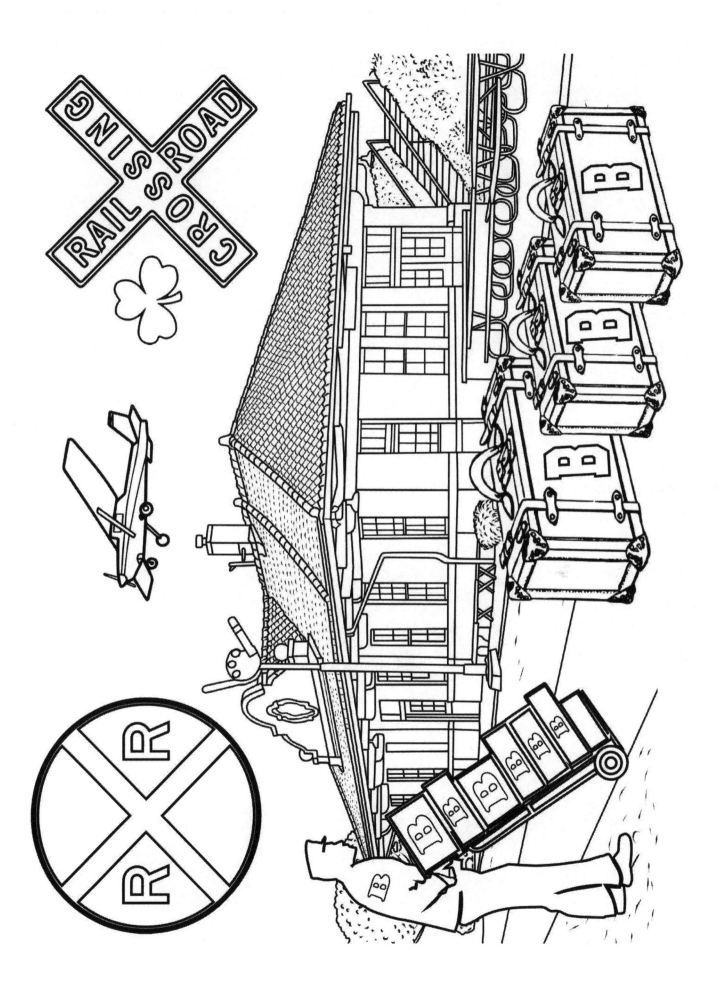

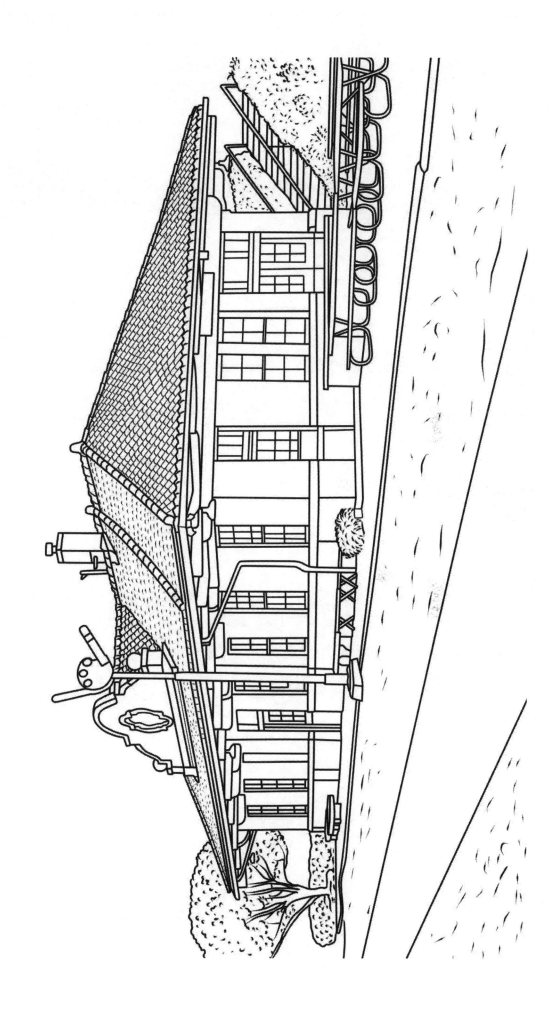

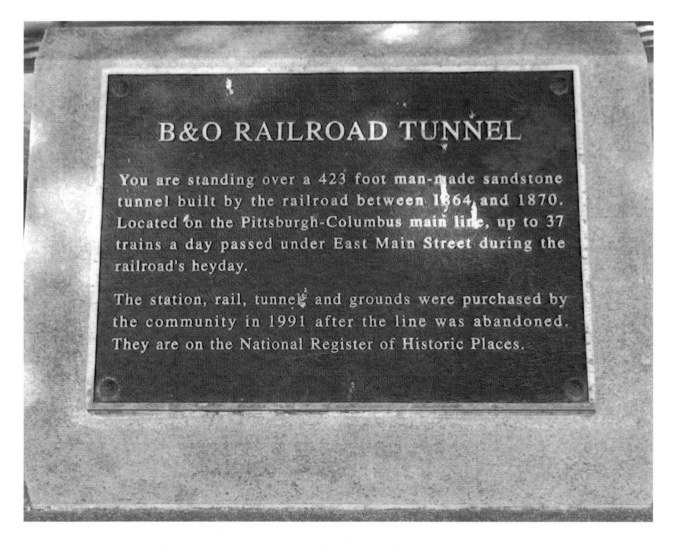

How many towns have their very own "Liars Bench" ?

I WILL ALWAYS BE A SHAMROCK

The next 6 pages contain 121 names of the streets of Barnesville, Ohio. 117 of them are real. 4 of them are made up. See if you can find the fictional streets.

Mt. Olivett

Line Grace Ridge Hunts
South Chestnut Street
W. Walnut St.
W. Walnut St. Libby Lane
South Broadway
Stadium North
Westview Pine Lane
Mulberry Bond
Carl Mill
West Main Street

South ☘ Arch Street ☘

GRAND VIEW

Law S OLNEY HILLS

WARREN IP BAILEY ROBINSON

KENNARD I HIGHLAND GREY

CARRIE IE BRENNON T

Bernhard ID A

DORSEY IE CLIFTON LEGGETT

HUTCHINSON L C McMILLAN

BELVIEW WOODLAND O MORRIS

A CLINTON

ROOSEVELT

 # SKI

BARNESVILLE AIRPORT
ONE-MILE WEST OF HOSPITAL

TOW—

4:00 to 10:00 Week Days—10:00 to 10:00 Saturdays

12:00 to 10:00 Sundays & Holidays

SKI RENTAL — SNO MOBILE RENTAL

FREE INSTRUCTION—RUTH GILLESPIE

SKI SCHOOL

SNO CONDITIONS

NORTH CHESTNUT STREET
North Broadway
E. Walnut St. Wiley
Church St. Jagger
Sycamore Park St.
B
Euclid E Watt L Lincoln Depot
PIKE L
Cherry St.
East Main Street
Washington

Deer at the backyard bird feeders are a common sight in Barnesville.

GREENMONT

Dusty
Fair St.
Walton
Reva
Cole Alaina Ave.
Brill Kirk High Pleasant
Shannon Road Franklin Fowler

O Jackson's Crossing
Sandy Ridge
A Homestead
Slabtown
K South St. Maple
· Shady Lane

Show off your work!

When you color a page, take a picture with your phone and send it to my phone 740-213-3789

or post it on the facebook page "Barnesville Ohio Coloring Book"

or email it to me and I will post it.
michealduve56@gmail.com

The next few pages contain images of the Bradfield Building that was home to the First National Bank of Barnesville for many years.

Built in 1891, making it 126 years old at the time of this printing, it has many unique architectural detail that some of you may not have been aware of.

I know I never noticed them until I took pictures with a digital camera and was able to enlarge them on a computer.

There are stone carvings of Gargoyles or monsters all over the building. After 126 years of weathering, they are a bit difficult to make out.

I have had them converted into line drawings to make them easier to see and to color. I hope you enjoy them.

These Two Monsters Sit atop the Pillars on either side of the West facing door.

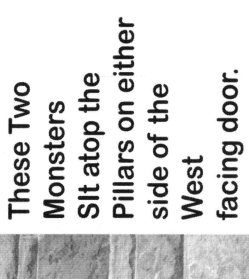

These two beauties guard the corners of the window nearest the door on the West facing side of the building. Bring these dull images to life with some brilliant colors.

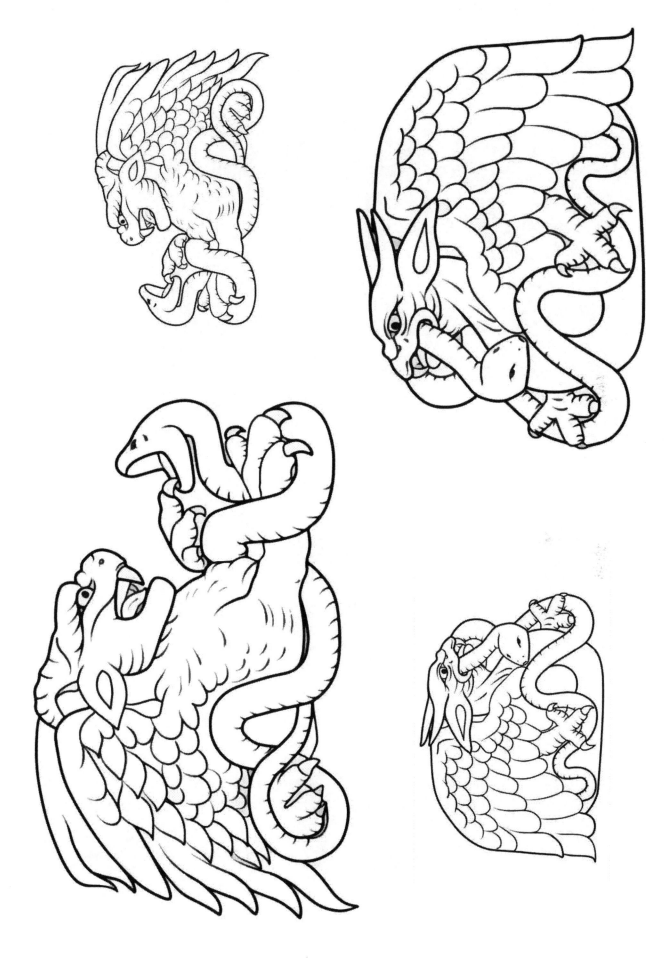

These two duling monsters have been locked in battle for more than a centruy. They are perched above the front door to the right Facing South.

Monsters gurard the First National Bank Building on the corner of Main and Chestnut St.

On the South side of the building above and to the right of the door between the windows.

On the Southwest Corner. Monster looks down on Main and Chestnut Streets.

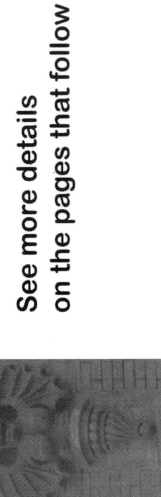

On the Northwest corner or back of the building

See more details on the pages that follow

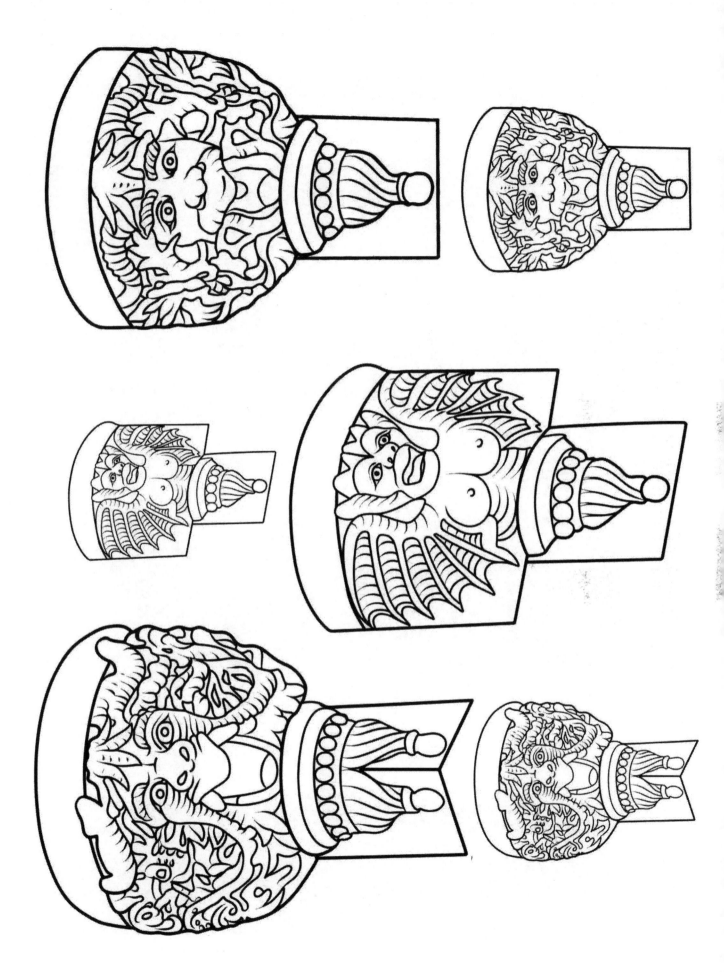

BRADFIELD BUILDING
BUILT IN 1891
FOR
FIRST NATIONAL BANK
EST. 1865
PRESENTED BY
BENJAMIN LUNDY QUESTERS
1990

Our Southeastern Ohio Nighborhood

Fairpoint ST. CLAIRSVILLE
NEW ATHENS Flushing Morristown
Sewellsville Laferty Bethesda
Fairview HENDRESBURG BELMONT
Quaker City BARNESVILLE
Salesville Malaga Warnock
Batesville Somerton Bealsville
SENACAVILLE Woodsfield Jerusalem

No Matter Where I Roam BARNESVILLE Will Always Be MY HOME

Terry "Butch" McKelvey and his Carp's Sunoco Dirt Track Race Car

FILLIN' UP THE TANK

Derry's 66 Station
ED'S TEXACO
Shafer's Hilltop Sinclair
Bill's TEXACO
SHORTY'S ASHLAND STATION
PURE OIL STATION
Carpenter's Sunoco
Don Hunter's Texaco
SKINNER'S GAS N GLO
Windland's Laundromat and Gas
PIERSOL'S SOHIO
Fusek's SHELL Station

Dave Hissom: 43 YEARS in the same location! Pumping gas and repairing cars.

Entertainment

THE MOOSE   The Ohio Theater
Leatherwood Drive In Theater
BINGO in The Catholic Church Basement
Albert George Youth Center
Memorial Park Pool
Hutton Memorial Library
State Movie Theater
George's Pool Hall
BUMMY'S POOL HALL

LEATHERWOOD DRIVE-IN THEATER

Route 147 — Barnesville, Ohio

NOW SHOWING — THRU SAT., AUG. 8

ALFRED HITCHCOCK'S

"TOPAZ"

plus

"SKULLDUGGERY"

SUN. THRU TUES. AUG. 9-10-11

CLINT EASTWOOD DOUBLE FEATURE

"THE GOOD, THE BAD and THE UGLY"

and

"HANG 'EM HIGH"

COMING: "Two Mules for Sister Sara" and "Eye of the Cat"

What Card Games Did You Learn To Play In Barnesville?

- SPADES
- 500 Rummy
- HEARTS
- CANASTA
- TONK
- Bolivia
- CINCH
- BRIDGE
- POKER
- PINOCHLE
- EUCHRE
- TRIPOLI

BET YOU KEPT SCORE WITH A PENCIL AND PAPER TOO. NO COMPUTERS NECESSARY TO HAVE FUN.

Show off your work!
When you color a page, take a picture with your phone and send it to my phone 740-213-3789 or post it on the facebook page "Barnesville Ohio Coloring Book" or email it to me and I will post it.
michealduve56@gmail.com

BANKING & INSURANCE

THE FIRST NATIONAL BANK OF BARNESVILLE

The People's Building and Loan

Peters Insurance

Hilda Truax Insurance

Hinkle Insurance

Hanlon Insurance

DRY CLEANING

BARNESVILLE DRY CLEANING

"Quality & Service Since 1931"

Drive-In — Downtown

146 W. MAIN ST.

Call

FEED AND SUPPLIES

GIBSON FEED & SUPPLY

- Grinding
- Molasses Mixing
- Fencing
- Animal Health Products
- Paint
- Feeds
- Fertilizer
- Pet Supplies
- Insecticides
- Dairy Supplies

CALL 425-

242 S. GARDNER ST.

RETAIL BUSINESSES

ARMSTRONG's JEWELRY THREE BLIND MICE

Moores Store   The Needle Nook

Gilbert's Men & Boys Wear   Hallmark House

G.C. MURPHY'S 5 AND 10 CENT STORE

George Cheffy's Men's Store   Roe's Home & Garden

East End Garage

Walter Thomas   The Flower Gardens and Greenhouse

Keystone Shoe Store

BARNESVILLE RETAIL SHOPPING

The Mayfair Miller Furniture

DAVIS JEWELERS

Fosters Finnical Drugs

McGhee's Nursery Western Auto

POLENS Kirks Polmatier's

Kenneady's Hardware The News Stand

SHEPHERD'S DRUGS

KV STORE Householder's Furniture

Bob Howell Power Equipment

ACKERMAN'S GUN & JEWELRY Barbara's

Fur Feather & Fin
PET AND TACK SHOP
330 SOUTH CHESTNUT STREET
BARNESVILLE, OHIO
425-3395

"ONE OF THE FINEST & MOST COMPLETE IN THE OHIO VALLEY"

Christmas Special
CHILDREN'S DENIM BOOTS

Reg. $16.95 **Special $11.95**

Blue Sueded cowhide foot and Blue Denim top.
- PVC platform outsole
- Snoot Toe
- Western Heel

SIZES: D Widths 9 thru 3

BELTS - BILLFOLDS - BOOTS
WESTERN SHIRTS
SIMCO LEATHER COATS
DENIM JEANS
MEN'S & LADIES' CASUAL
WESTERN SUITS
DENIM JACKETS
CORDUROY WESTERN PANTS
HATS BOOT SOCKS
SADDLES & TACK
NEW SHIPMENT WESTERN
BELT BUCKLES
TURQUOISE JEWELRY
— 1/3 OFF —

FISH SPECIALS

Red Moons . . . . 3/$1.00

Black Mollies . . 3/$1.00

Rasboras . . . . 2/$1.00

Green Swords . . 2/$1.00

AKC PUPPIES IN STOCK

Brittany Spaniels
Dachshunds
Pekingese
Toy Poodles
Lhasa Apsos
Australian Terriers

Layaway Now For Christmas

Dining in Old Barnesville

The Plaza Restaurant

Schafer's Restaurant

Okay's Dairy Bar

The Green Cottage

Bohandy's

Harp's

Hall's Drive In

The Green Castle

HOME PIZZA

Pizza Rack

Thompson's Frosty Treat

Hunkler's Restaurant

D-Oro Inn

Truax Testaurant

Bell s

OUR JANUARY CLEARANCE will keep you warm

Men's & Boys' JACKETS
ALL OUT SAVINGS
Reduced 20%

DRESS GLOVES REDUCED 20%

GREAT SALE... COATS
ALL WEATHER COATS — Reduced 20%
TOPCOATS Reduced 25%

Clearance SWEATERS
MEN'S and BOYS' REDUCED 20%

Bank the Savings — SUIT CLEARANCE
MEN'S and BOYS' REDUCED 10%

CLEARANCE OF SHOES — SAVE SAVE SAVE
Ladies Winter Dress Shoes REDUCED 20%

Walter Thomas

ICE CREAM
BARNESVILLE OHIO
TOP QUALITY SINCE 1855

There is nothing complicated with our

5%

Certificate of Deposit

$1,000.00 Minimum

6 Month Maturity

Renewal Automatic

Interest by Check or Credit

FDIC Insurance Now $20,000.00

First **NATIONAL BANK** —OF— BARNESVILLE

Plus Complete Banking Services

BARNESVILLE   BETHESDA

Looking Your Best in Old Barnesville

Stonebraker's Barber Shop

Talk of The Town Beauty Shop

Ruby's Beauty Salon

Don's Barber Shop

Inn-Styles Beauty Salon

Twins Beauty Shop

Adeline's Beauty Shop

Floyd Wilcox Barber Shop

The Beauty Nook   Doc's Barber Shop

MINING CAR WHEEL Co.

MANUFACTURERS OF

MINE and ORE CARS
of Every Description
CAR WHEELS and
AXLES
MINE CARS COMPLETE

WATT Patent Self-Oiling
Mine Car Wheels
WATT Patent Channel
Bar Attachment For
Round Axles

BARNESVILLE OHIO USA

R.R. Watt Pres. and Gen Mgr.
J.J. Watt Vice Pres. and Treas.

Local
& Long Distance
Telephone No. 11

PROFESSIONAL SERVICES

H.C. Plumly Excavating

BUNDY'S RADIO AND TV

Broomhall Builders

Ralph King Taylor & Stockbroker

Cook's Typewriters

Miller's Shoe Repair

Rohrbach Brother's Garage

Murphy's Gifts for the Entire Family

CHRISTMAS SHOP WHERE SELECTIONS ARE LARGE & PRICES ARE LOW...SEE

3 DAYS ONLY!
DECEMBER 17, 18, 19

HEY KIDS
Santa Will Be At Murphy's
Thursday - Friday - Monday
5:30 - 8:30
Sat. 1 to 4 & 5 to 8

"STERLING PORTABLE"
TYPEWRITER
Blue vinyl clad carrying case, 88 character keyboard, tab touch selector, quickset margins plus 2 year guarantee.
Reg. $77.84
67.84
CHARGE IT

Our Own Carolina Moon Carol-Ions or Agilon
PANTY HOSE $1.57 pr.
Carol-Ions is 100% Polyamide II stretch fibre, in many colors and sizes. Agilon's micromesh, seamless in 5 shades & many sizes.
Regular $1.77

2 prs $3

Our Own Carole Joanne Polyester & Cotton
BLOUSES $2.99 each
Permanent Press. Cuffed short sleeves. Convertible Collar, 26" length. Green, Gold, Beige, White, Blue, Pink. 30/38.

BOY'S PLAID
C.P.O. SHIRT $6.99
45% Reprocessed Wool 40% Wool and 15% Nylon. Flap Pockets. Sizes S-M-L

MEN'S PERMANENT PRESS. WHITE & COLORS 2.57 each
LONG SLEEVE DRESS SHIRT 2 For $5.00

MEN'S COTTON AND POLYESTER, FANCY or SOLIDS 3.57 each
NO-IRON PAJAMAS 2 For $7.00

BOY'S PULLOVER
ACRYLIC SWEATERS $3.94

BIG 4 POUND BOX
THURMAN'S CREAMY
CHOCOLATES
Reg. 3.47
BOX **$2.94**

---

mince O matic
AS SEEN ON TV

IT'S A:
- MINCER
- CHOPPER
- BLENDER
- GRATER
- RICER
- JUICER
- FOOD MILL
- ICE CRUSHER
- ONION MINCER
- HASH MAKER
- POTATO GRATER

NOW ONLY **$5.99**

VEG-O-MATIC
AS SEEN ON TV

Get yours here for
Only **$7.77**

The Most Revolutionary Kitchen Appliance of the Century!

SLICES...
DICES...
WHOLE FOODS IN JUST ONE STROKE!

FASTER than an electric machine! Pepper... WHOLE Potatoes... Tomatoes... Cucumbers... Onions... Hardboiled Eggs! Makes thick slices or thin slices. Slices a WHOLE ONION in one stroke... every slice perfect!

POLAROID COLORPACK II CAMERA
$29.95 VALUE
Our Low Price **$24.97**
Easy to use. Takes Color or Black & White.
Polacolor type 108 Film only $3.97

AT MURPHY'S "CHARGE IT" WITH BANK CHARGE CARD

Open 9 to 9 'Til Dec. 24

G. C. MURPHY CO. - First Quality Always

PROFESSIONAL SERVICES

Barnesville Dry Cleaning

Red Loper's TAXI

Crum's Body Shop   88 CAB

Davis Recycling

Miles Curtis Hauling   Grier's TAXI

Buss Warren Indian Cycle Shop

Carl Hollingsworth's Barnesville Welding Shop

Whiteley Studio of Photography

GROCERIES AND MORE

HILLTOP CARRYOUT

Boyd's Market　ROBY'S　Mayo's Grocery

LELA HOUSE GROCERY　GILL'S M+K

Handy Candy　MADELYN'S CARRYOUT

Garvin's Dairy Store　Steele's Grocery

ROCKWELL ORCHARDS　Finche's Grocery

Larry's M&K

Mantz's Bakery　FOGLE'S BAKERY

Binn's IGA　REICH'S MEAT MARKET

Van Dyne's Super Market

HERB HALL GROCERY

Moore's Meats　DAIRY MART

Ralph's Super Market　Lawson's

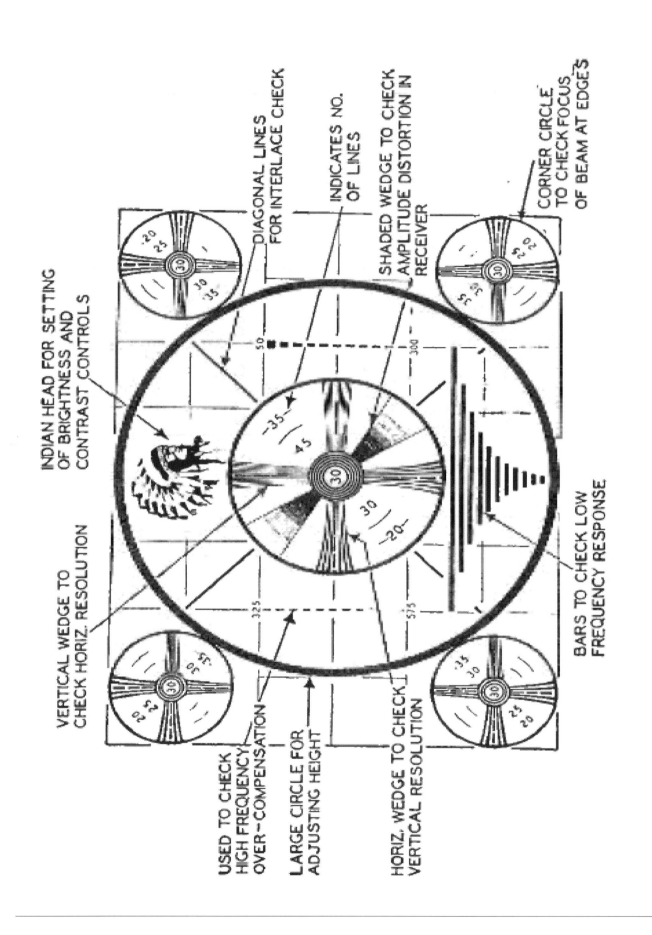

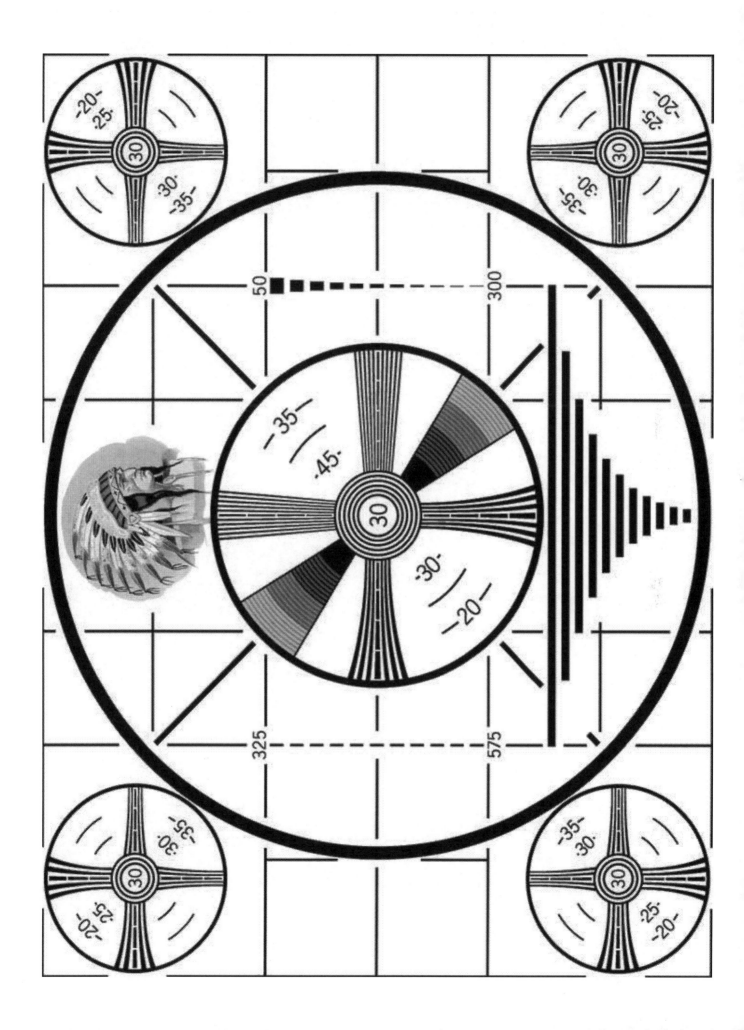

CABLE TV IS COMING TO BARNESVILLE

SUBSCRIPTION SALES NOW UNDERWAY

Special Introductory Offer

FREE Installation and 30 Day FREE Trial

$5.00 Monthly Service Charge After First 30 Days

Offer Good To April 15, 1970

---

10 Channels of Quality Reception

Channel 2 KDKA Pittsburgh (CBS)
Channel 4 WTAE Pittsburgh (ABC)
Channel 7 WTRF Wheeling (NBC/ABC)
Channel 9 WSTV Steubenville (CBS/ABC)
Channel 11 WIIC Pittsburgh (NBC)
Channel 13 WQED Pittsburgh (Educational)
Channel 18 WHIZ Zanesville (ABC/NBC)
Channel 20 WOMB Athens (Educational)
Channel 53 WPGH Pittsburgh (Independent)
Time and Weather Channel

Also: BROAD BAND FM SERVICE

After April 15
Installation Fee $10.00 — Monthly Service $5.00

HOMELITE XLs are the fastest selling chain saws in the world!

HOMELITE® XL-12

Over half a million XL chain saws built and sold.

- Weighs only 13¼ lbs. dry less bar and chain
- Easy to start—easy to handle
- Fells trees up to 3 feet in diameter

Get a free demonstration today!

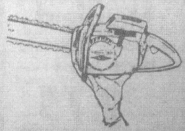

Bob Howell
Power Equipment
124 Sycamore St.
Phone 425-

PIERSOL SOHIO
SERVICE

- Brake Service   • Exhausts
- Complete Tune Up
- Wheel Balancing
- Atlas Tires . Batteries & Accessories.

WINTER TIRES
Still at Special Prices

HOURS
7:00 A.M. till 10:00 P.M.

425-

CHURCH & CHESTNUT STS.

Manufacturing and Industrial

Campus Shirts   B&O Depot   OHIO POWER

Johathan Logan Factory   POMCO   TIDY CAR

Sampson's Cash & Carry Lumber

Watt Car & Wheel   The Whetstone

R & R Trucking   5 B'S   Ault Automotive

Lotus Glass   KINNEY MOTOR COMPANY

C & L Auto Parts

OHIO BELL TELEPHONE   Damsel's Ice Cream

Barnesville Manufacturing

ALBERT BEANS HILLTOP AUTO PARTS   BOB S CHEVROLET

BARNESVILLE AUTO SUPPLY   UNITED DAIRY

Peters Motors

DEVINE HARLEY - DAVIDSON

Dalton's Tire Shop   Barnesville Lumber

Barnesville Motors   SMITH LUMBER

Gibson Feed & Supply   Belmont Tire

HASTING'S FEED MILL   WELL'S COAL

Skinner's Dairy   HANLON PAPER CO.

**Grand Opening of "Bob Howell Power Equipment"
November 1959
Pictured Left to Right:
Bob Howell, his Wife Bea,
Daughters: Betty Ann, Barbara Jean,
and in front Helen Jane and Bobbie Carol.**

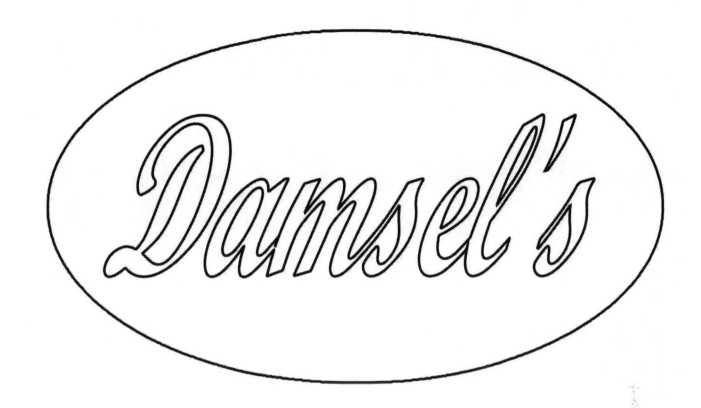

ICE CREAM
BARNESVILLE OHIO
TOP QUALITY SINCE 1855

The Morel Mushroom is a delicacy that grows wild in the Barnesville area. Usually harvested in early spring. >>>>>>>>>>>>>>>>>>>>>>>>>>>>>>>

Remember this trick question? How many groves are there on a 33 1/3 rpm LP vinyl record album?

Answer.... on next page..

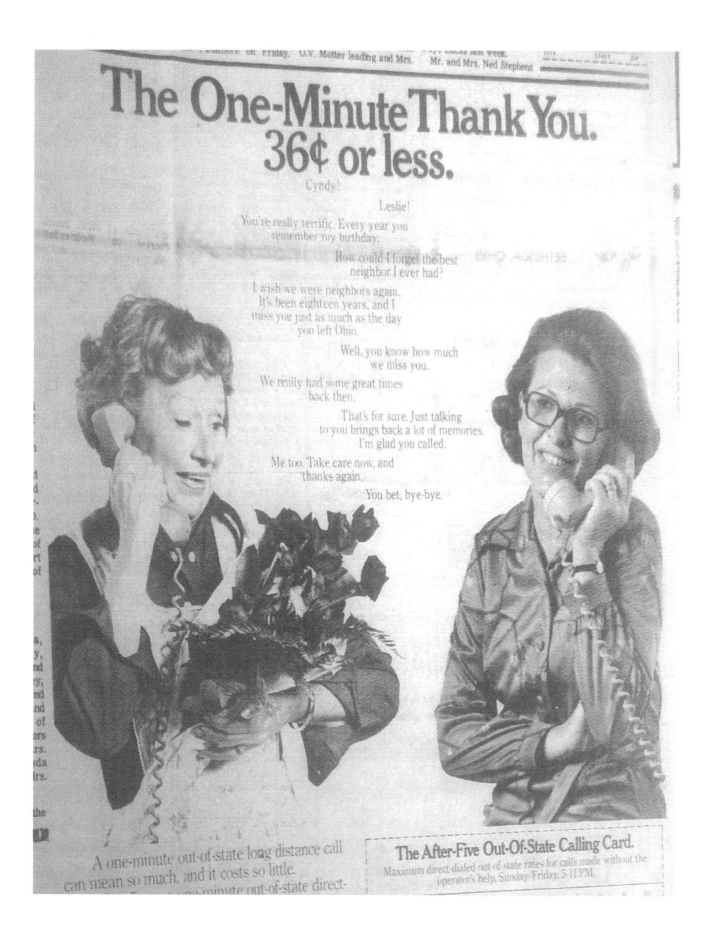

There is ONE continuous grove on all vinyl records.

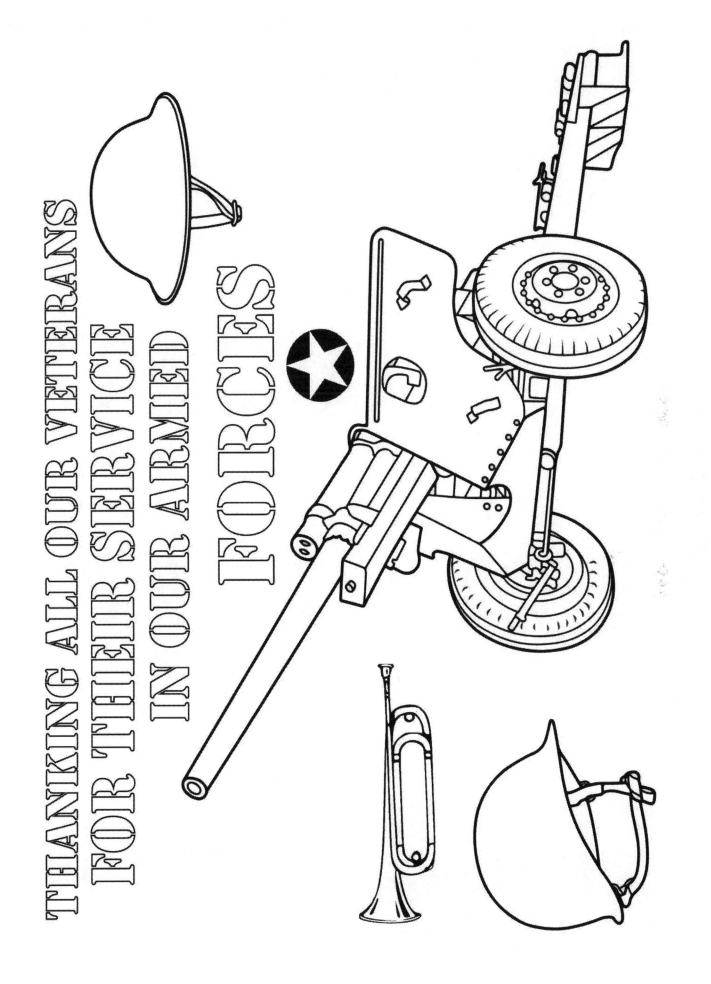

The Beautiful Birds of Barnesville.
Adding color to our sky. >>>>>>>>>

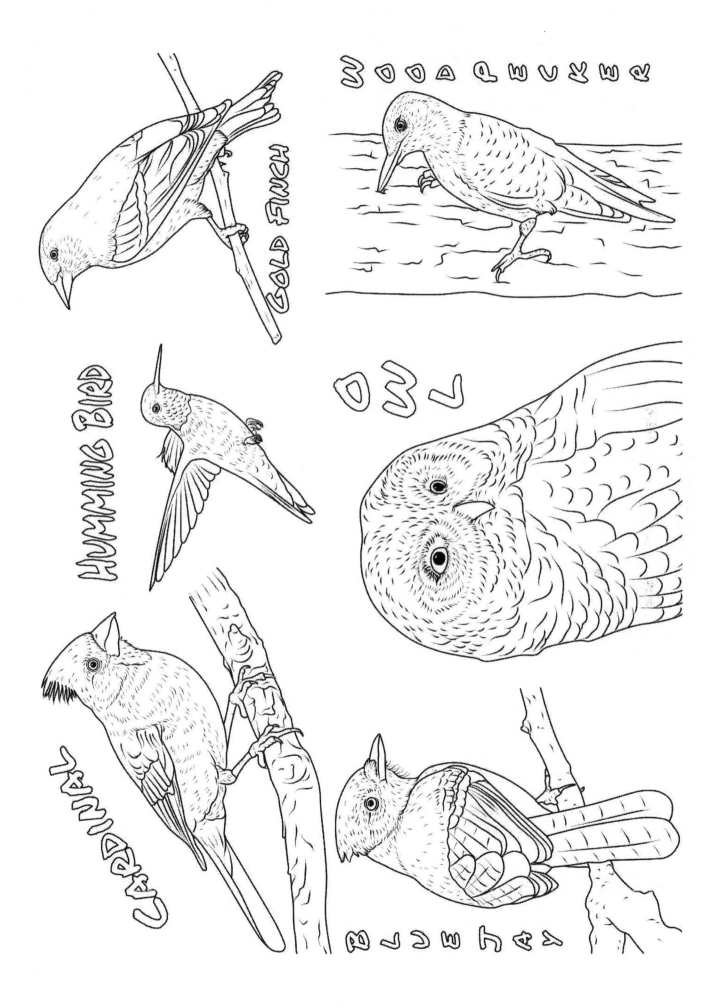

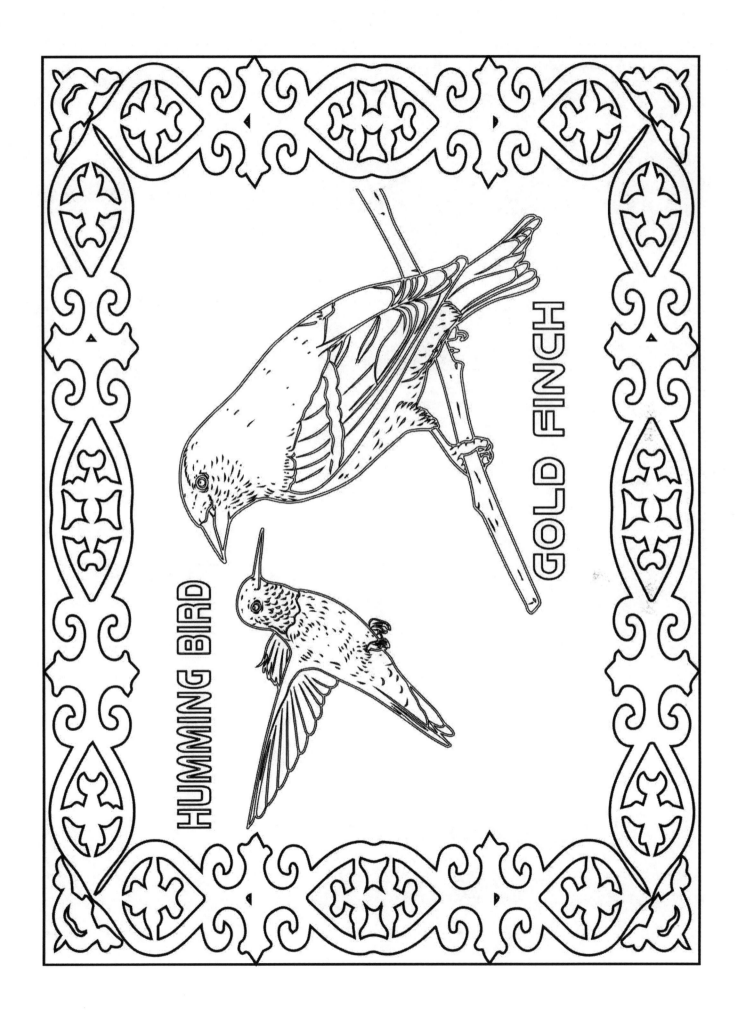

Show off your work!

When you color a page, take a picture with your phone and send it to my phone 740-213-3789

or post it on the facebook page "Barnesville Ohio Coloring Book"

or email it to me and I will post it. michealduve56@gmail.com

Have the Winter BLAHS???

Tired of winter? Tired of the same old look? Come see us for a new style and cut!

TWINS
Beauty Shop
Phone 425-▮
168 East Main St.

McGHEES NURSERY

Christmas Trees & Cemetery Arrangements

Long Needle Cut .... $3.00 & up

Norway Spruce Cut .. $3.00 & up

Douglas Fir .... $2.00 & up

Grave Blankets, Pillows & Mounds

Bundles of Cut Pine & Roping

You Cut Norway Spruce from field .... 4-10 ft. .... $3.00 ea.

Henderson Street
South of Dairy Queen
Phone 425-▮
BARNESVILLE, OHIO

12-3-10

DOLLAR DAYS

PACK OF 100 PLASTIC FORKS & SPOONS	39¢
PLASTIC DUST PANS	19¢
CAR SEAT CUSHION WIRE and FIBRE	99¢
3 PAIRS NYLONS - Reg. 69¢	3 Pairs $1.00
100 - 5 gr. McKESSON ASPIRIN	23¢
79¢ MENNEN - COLGATE - AERSOL SHAVE CREAM	47¢
HAIR SETTING GEL - Reg. 2.50	73¢
A P C (Aanacin Formula) Reg. 49¢ 25's	25¢
SCHOOL NOTEBOOK FILLER PAPER 300 SHEETS	57¢
25¢ BALL POINT YES PENS	13¢

CHECK OUR CLEARANCE TABLE

FINNICAL DRUGS

BRINGING THE HORSE AND BUGGY BACK TO BARNESVILLE

JUST IMAGINE WHEN EVERYONE IN TOWN GOT AROUND THIS WAY

Horse of a Different Color?

The Belmont County Victorian Mansion Museum. >>>>>>>>>>>>>>>>>>>>>>>>>>>

Located at 532 North Chestnut Street.

Featuring 26 rooms of historical elegance.

Construction began in 1888 and was completed in 1893.

Inside you will find superbly carved Oak fretwork, bathrooms of marble with gold trim, hundreds of historical artifacts, and so much more.

This is a local site not to be missed!

Visit and "Take a Step Back In Time".

For tours and information, please call: 740-425-2926

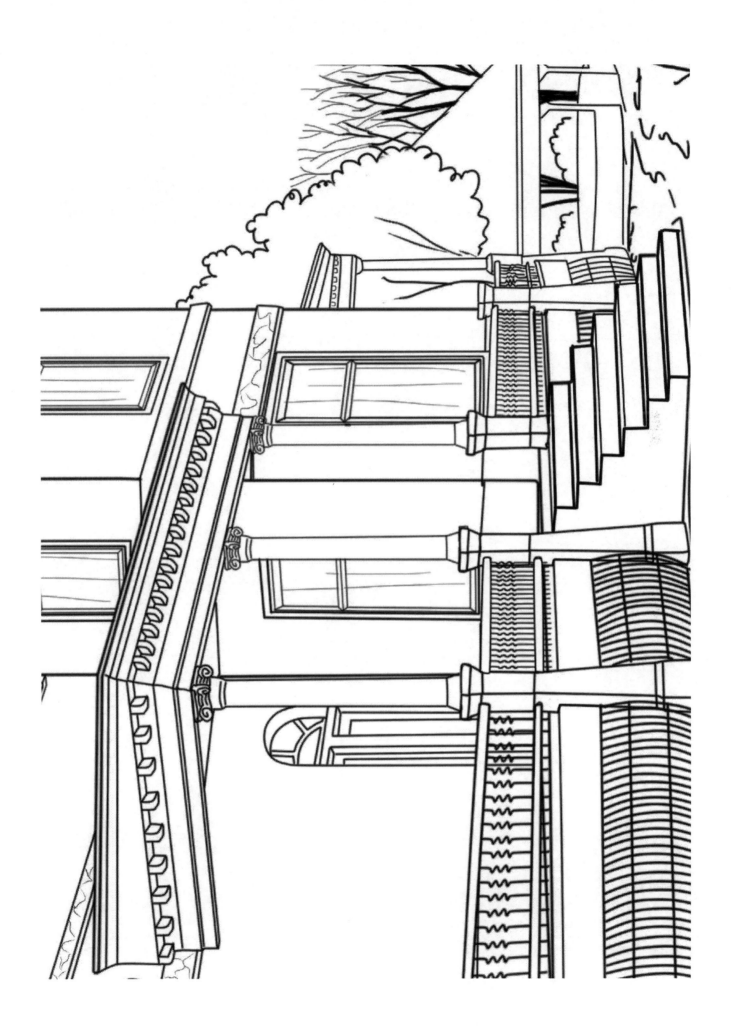

BETTY'S BEAUTY PARLOR

512 N. LINCOLN

To Our Customers:

Appointments not necessary during day.

Every month we will award 5 Free Shampoo and Sets, and one Free Permanent Wave. Only our Customers may register.

SHAMPOO & SETS - Modern Styles .... $2. & up

PERMANENT WAVES .... $8 - $10 - $12.50 & up

Frostings — $12.50;   Manicures - Eyebrow Arches

WIGLETS Washed and Set $3.00

WIGS Washed and Set $5.00

— OPERATORS —

Debbie McWilliams - Becky Howell - Betty Wehr

Evenings by Appointment

BARNESVILLE - BRADFIELD AIRPORT

ELEVATION 1312 FEET

N 40.00-08.7000 N
W 081-11-30.6000 W

In Memory of
Clyde "Sheets" Wittenbrook

I thought this image reminded me of airplane propellers or jet engine fan blades. >>>>>>

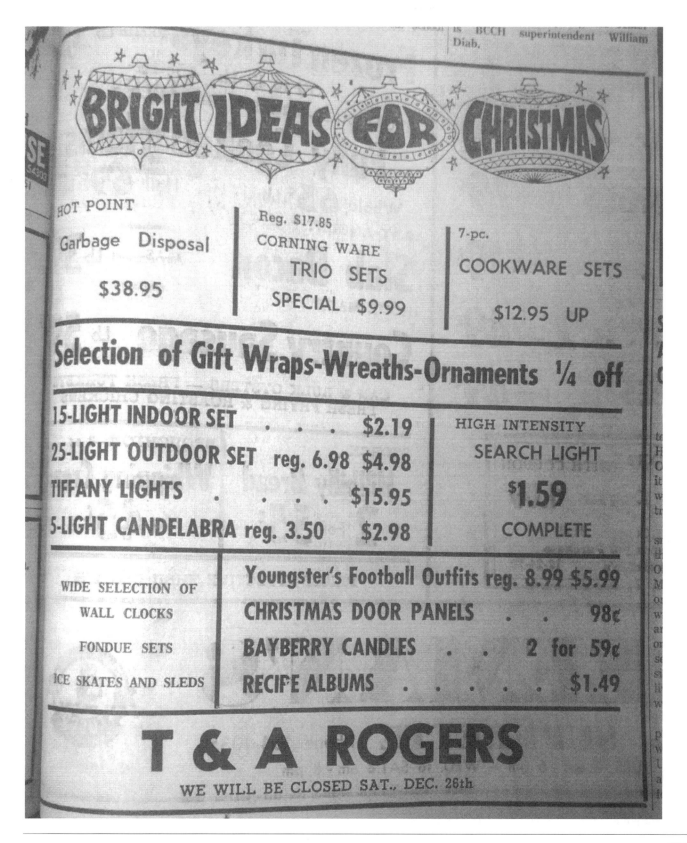

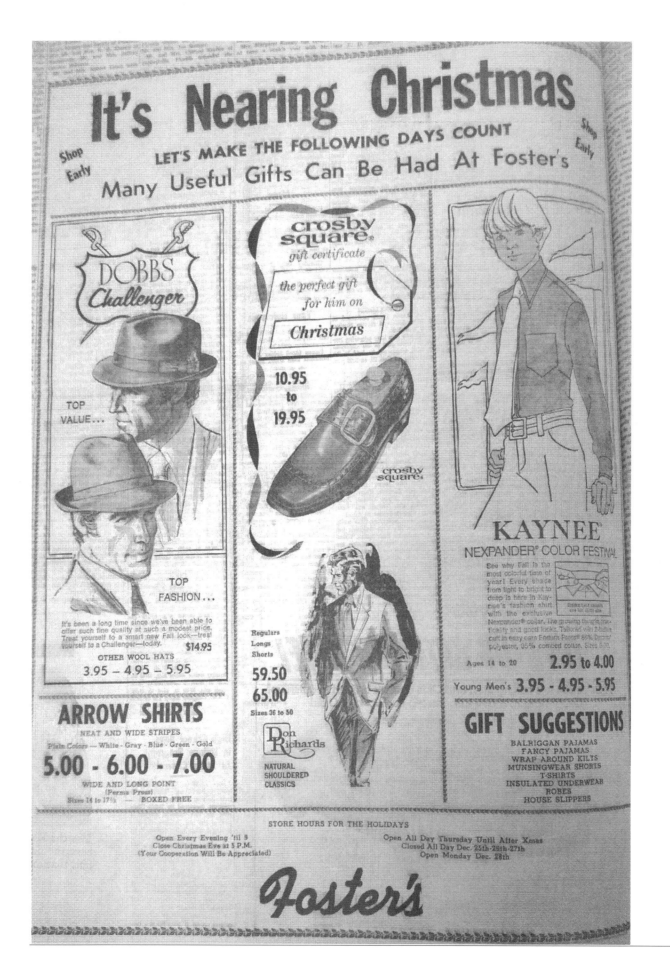

Famous Local Fisherman Bill Duve

It wouldn't be Summer In Barnesville Without a LOT of

YARD SALE →

YARD SALE TODAY!

3 FAMILY YARD SALE

GARAGE SALE

BIG YARD SALE

The Barnesville Pumpkin Festival. Began in 1964 in the basement of the Church of The Assumption.

Over the years, the Pumpkin Festival has attracted hundreds of thousands of visitors to Barnesville.

Always held on the last full weekend of September. Beginning Wednesday night with the weigh in of the giant pumpkins and the crowning of the "KING PUMPKIN".

Featuring the big parade on Saturday afternoon.

Filling several downtown streets with agricultural displays and plenty of food, games, and rides.

Plenty of Pumpkin Bread, Pumpkin Ice Cream and more.

They found a perch to watch the parade from.

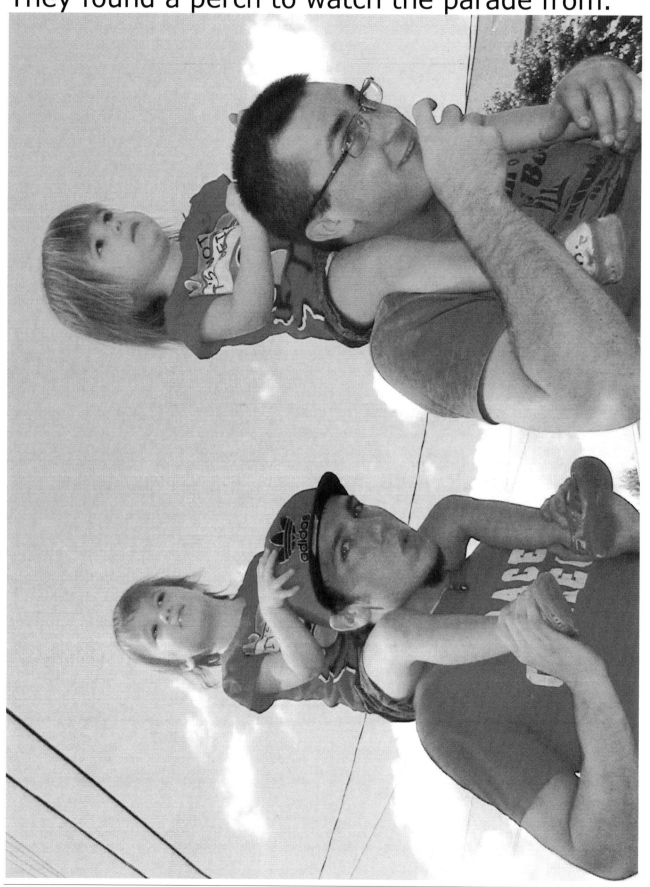

Pumpkin Festival
Memories
Pumpkin Coming Home
Pumpkin Wagon
Old Big Smiles
Family Reunions
Friends
Pumpkin Ice Cream
King Pumpkin Weigh In
The Big Parade
Tall Tales

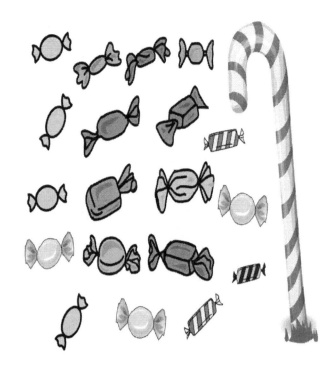

**Candy in the Street.
Candy in the Air
Candy Everywhere... Yeaaaaaaaaa**

- Pumpkin Festival
- Memories
- Pie Baking Contest
- Antique Cars
- Cattlemen's Ribeye Sandwich
- Beard and Moustache Contest
- Vintage Tractors
- Apple Dumplings
- Pie Eating Contest
- Games

The GEM of Egypt. The 1950-B Model Shovel built by Bucyrus-Erie near Milwaukee WI. in 1966.

GEM stands for Giant Excavating Machine or Giant Earth Mover. Depending on what source you use.

Egypt for the Hanna Coal Company Egypt Valley Mine near Barnesville where it began working in February of 1967.

In order to build I-70 across land owned by the Hanna Coal company. The State of Ohio, in 1964 agreed to allow Hanna up to 10 crossings of the Interstate over a 40 year period.

In 1972 the GEM was scheduled to cross I-70 at Hendrysburg, but instead, they moved the smaller Mountaineer and 46A shovels.

A 6 foot tall mound of crushed stone and earth was placed over I-70 and traffic was detoured while the shovels crossed to the other side.

In less than 24 hours, the move was complete. The interstate was cleared, cleaned and traffic restored. Evidence of the work done by the GEM and the other shovels can still be seen today.
The GEM was parked in 1988 between New Athens and Fairpoint and scrapped in 1991.

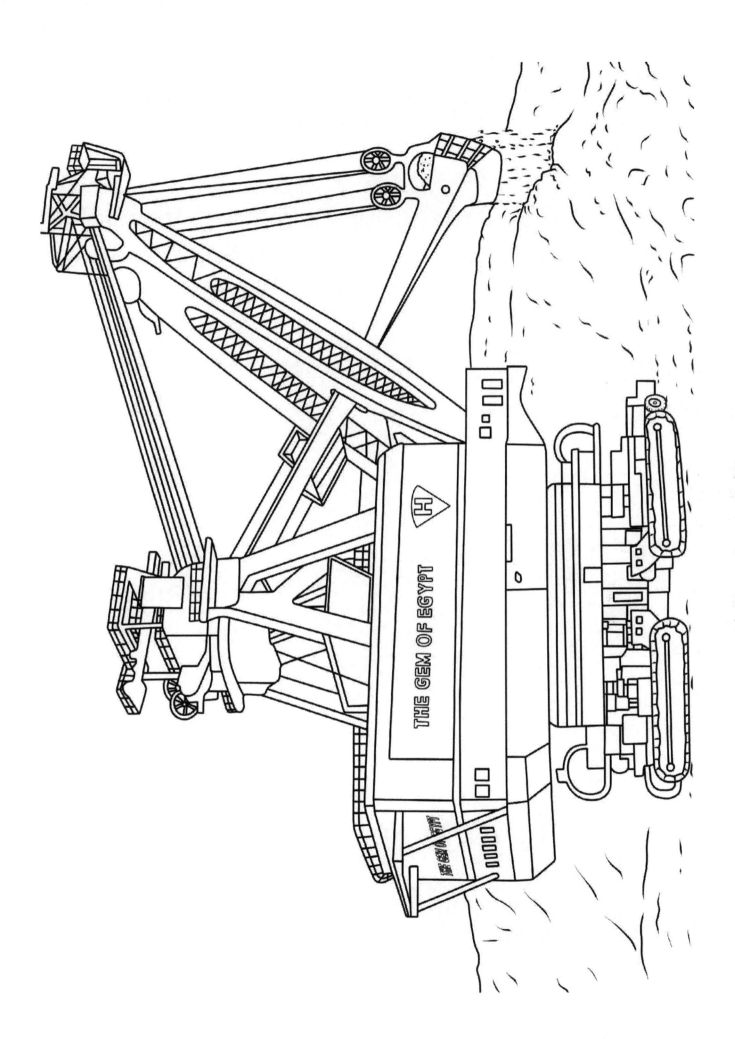

Show off your work!

When you color a page, take a picture with your phone and send it to my phone 740-213-3789

or post it on the facebook page "Barnesville Ohio Coloring Book"

or email it to me and I will post it. michealduve56@gmail.com

WITH A TOTAL ELECTRIC

PIZZAZZ PERMANENT HOME
MORE QUALITY — MORE STYLE

LESS PRICE

BUY DIRECT FROM OUR FACTORY

IN BARNESVILLE

THE PIZZAZZ "Eight Fourty" 3 BED ROOM MODEL WITH FULL INSULATION, STORM SASH, & SCREENS, FULLY CARPETED, DECORATOR KITCHEN & BATH CABINETS PLUS CUSTOM BUILT-INS, COLOR MATCHING RANGE, HOOD, SINK & REFRIGERATOR, FULL BASEMENT WITH LAUNDRY HOOKUP ON YOUR LOT.

$14,500.

This Home complete with all painting, curtain rods, service lines to Barnesville Water & Sewer, Underground Electric, Pre-Wired Telephones, Lovely Landscaped 6000 sq. ft. lot, seeded with front walk, yard, light and distinctive Shade Deck in new Walton's Woods Restricted Development.

$17,500.
90% FINANCING

OPEN SUNDAY
ONE TO SEVEN

Laws St. By The Stadium Parking Lot

Restricted Walton's Woods

In Barnesville

AL SMITH & ASSOCIATES
DIVISION OF O. M. SMITH LUMBER

Remember when a trip to Elby's was a BIG DEAL ?

The Armstrong Jewelers Clock. >>>>>>

Still stands on Main Street and Still Keeps Time.

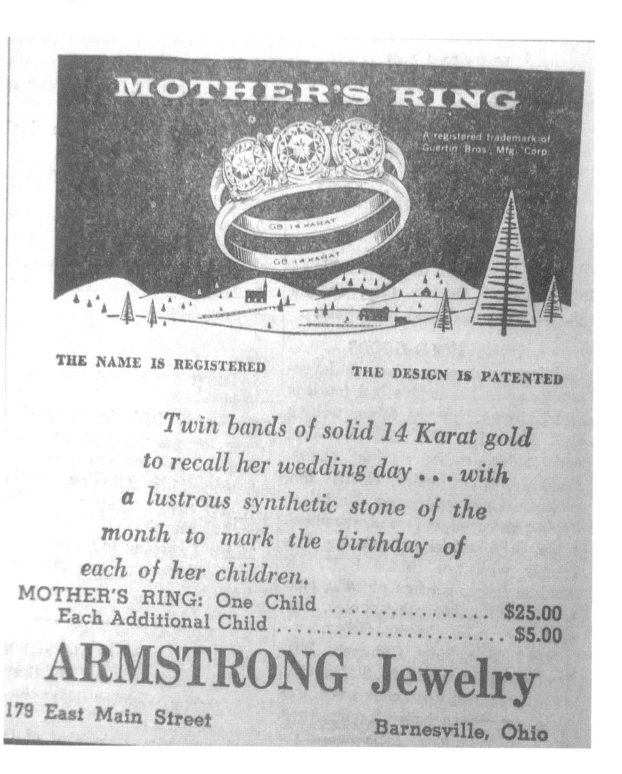

womp radio
The Friendly Giant

WOMP
Presents...

THE HOLIDAY SEASON IN SONG WEDNESDAY NOON THRU CHRISTMAS DAY

Brought To You In Part By:
GILBERT'S MEN'S WEAR
FUSEK'S SHELL SERVICE
SEAR'S CATALOG MERCHANT
DeVINE'S HARLEY DAVIDSON SALES
BOSWELL MONUMENTS
O.M. SMITH LUMBER
BARNESVILLE LUMBER

J-Mo's... what a great clock.

and ....

It's where all the

"Cattlemen's Ribeye" Sandwiches served during the Pumpkin Festival start out....

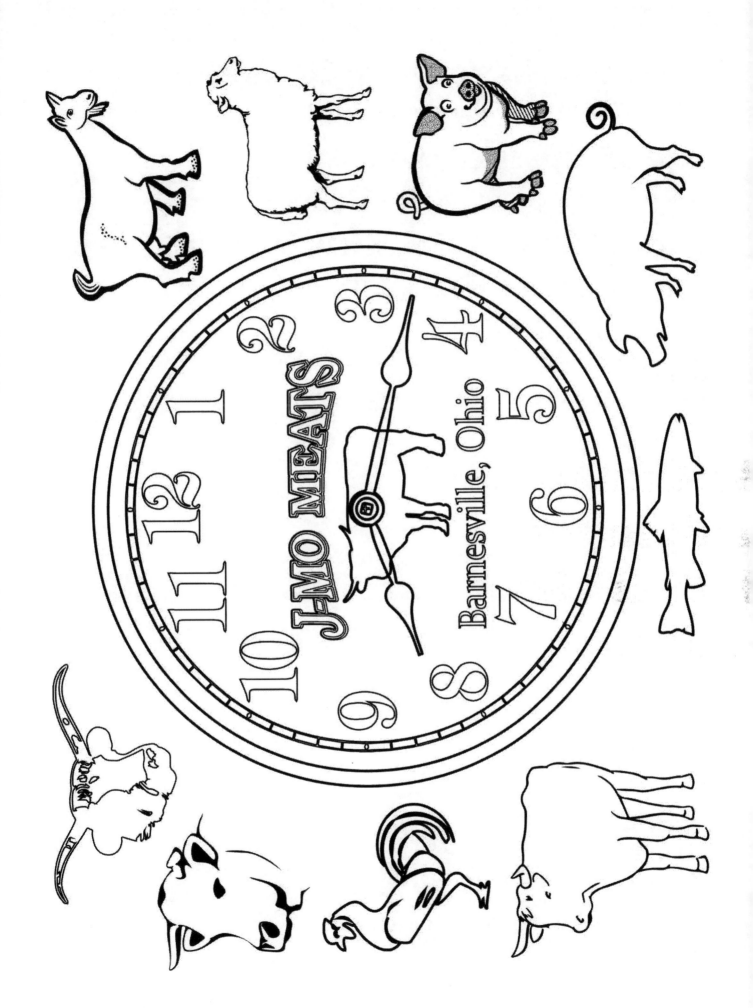

You may have thought the term "Snail Mail" wasn't coined until the age of the internet.

But, think again. This is an ad from the Barnesville Yellow Pages in the 1960's !!! >>>>>

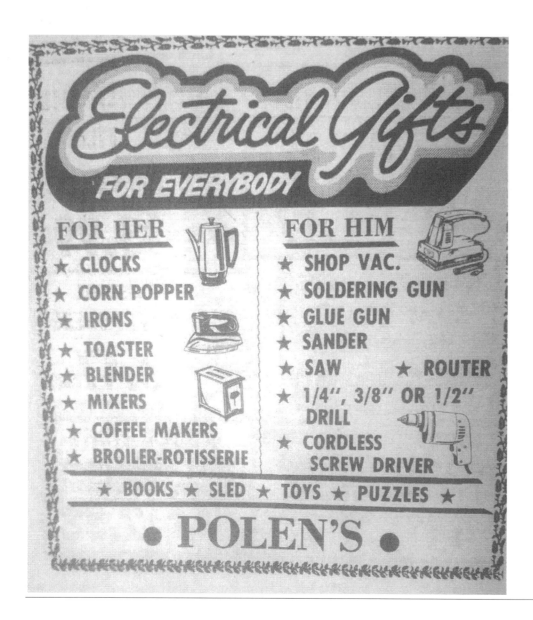

Do you have an interesting photograph of life in Barnesville that should be in the next edition of this book? Please let me know.

This Coloring Book can also be "CUSTOMIZED". I can add pictures of you, your family or business to any of the pages, for a truly "ONE OF A KIND" Gift.

Call or Text:
740-213-3789

LIFE IS SHORT

BUY THE SHOES

TAKE THE TRIP

SEE THE MOVIE

EAT THE CAKE

Show off your work!

When you color a page, take a picture with your phone and send it to my phone 740-213-3789

or post it on the facebook page "Barnesville Ohio Coloring Book"

or email it to me and I will post it.
michealduve56@gmail.com

For copies of this book:
Call or text 740-213-3789
Facebook at Barnesville Ohio Coloring Book
email: michaelduve56@gmail.com